D1071510

INVESTIGATE
Methamphetamine

Other titles in the  series:

Investigate
Alcohol
Library ISBN: 978-0-7660-4235-7
Paperback ISBN: 978-1-4644-0449-8

Investigate
Club Drugs
Library ISBN: 978-0-7660-4221-6
Paperback ISBN: 978-1-4644-0385-9

Investigate
Cocaine and Crack
Library ISBN: 978-0-7660-4255-1
Paperback ISBN: 978-1-4644-0453-5

Investigate
Methamphetamine
Library ISBN: 978-0-7660-4254-4
Paperback ISBN: 978-1-4644-0451-1

Investigate
Steroids and Performance Drugs
Library ISBN: 978-0-7660-4240-7
Paperback ISBN: 978-1-4644-0423-8

INVESTIGATE
Methamphetamine

INVESTIGATE

Marylou Ambrose
and
Veronica Deisler

Enslow Publishers, Inc.
40 Industrial Road
Box 398
Berkeley Heights, NJ 07922
USA

http://www.enslow.com

Library of Congress Cataloging-in-Publication Data

Ambrose, Marylou.
    Investigate methamphetamine / Marylou Ambrose and Veronica Deisler.
        pages cm. — (Investigate drugs)
    Includes bibliographical references and index.
    Summary: "Find out what methamphetamines are, what happens when someone be-
    comes addicted, and how the addiction is treated"— Provided by publisher.
    ISBN 978-0-7660-4254-4
    1. Methamphetamine—Juvenile literature. 2. Methamphetamine abuse—Juvenile lit-
    erature. I. Deisler, Veronica. II. Title.
    RC568.A45A53 2015
    616.86'4—dc23
                            2013008771

Future editions:
Paperback ISBN: 978-1-4644-0451-1   Single-User PDF ISBN: 978-1-4646-1245-9
EPUB ISBN: 978-1-4645-1245-2   Multi-User PDF ISBN: 978-0-7660-5877-4

Printed in the United States of America

062014 Lake Book Manufacturing, Inc., Melrose Place, IL

10 9 8 7 6 5 4 3 2 1

To Our Readers: We have done our best to make sure all Internet Addresses in this book were active and appropriate when we went to press. However, the author and the publisher have no control over and assume no liability for the material available on those Internet sites or on other Web sites they may link to. Any comments or suggestions can be sent by e-mail to comments@enslow.com or to the address on the back cover.

♻ Enslow Publishers, Inc., is committed to printing our books on recycled paper. The paper in every book contains 10% to 30% post-consumer waste (PCW). The cover board on the outside of each book contains 100% PCW. Our goal is to do our part to help young people and the environment too!

Photo Credits: Drug Enforcement Administration, p. 13; Library of Congress, pp. 32; 40; National Institute on Drug Abuse, pp. 17, 52; Photo taken by Dozenist/Wikipedia. com Public Domain Image, p. 19; Shutterstock: (©Zurijeta, p. 8; ©Zerbor, pp. 28–29; ©Anna Omelchenko, p. 43; ©Phase4Studios, p. 65; ©mangostock, p. 77; ©hikrcn, p. 55; antoshkaforever, p. 88); ©Thinkstock: (MihajloMaricic/iStock, p. 14; Devonyue/ iStock, p. 20; Jupiterimages/liquidlibrary, p. 23; iStock, p. 26; Fuse, p. 36; Andrea Danti/ Hemera, p. 48; kshevtsov/iStock, p. 55; HemeraTechnologies/ PhotoObjects.net, p. 58; Mark Herreid/iStock, p. 60; fatchoi/iStock, p. 74; monkeybusinessimages/iStock, p. 83; Jeff Golden Collection: Getty Images Sport, p. 91); United States Army, p. 30; U.S. Drug Enforcement Administration, pp. 42, 51; United States Marines, p. 34.

Cover Illustration: ©Thinkstock: diego/iStock

Contents

Introduction

It was the "feel good" drug that helped millions. It treated everyone from overweight women to hyperactive kids to people with depression or breathing problems. It was the choice of artists, writers, soldiers, athletes, and an American president.

It's a form of amphetamine. It gives people energy and makes them feel confident. But the good feelings don't last long. The drug's dark side makes people aggressive and hostile, it causes them to lie and steal, and it damages their bodies and brains. It's also highly addictive, destroys families, and costs society billions of dollars. It was even used by a crazed German leader who wanted to conquer the world. To some, it's the world's most dangerous drug—methamphetamine.

Drugs that "speed" people up are the most commonly abused drugs worldwide. They're also the most addictive. Meth is the strongest in this group, which means it can be the most harmful. There are 26 million meth addicts around the world today. Over a million of them live in the United States. They don't just "use" meth. They "abuse" it.

This book will give you the facts about meth. It describes what meth looks like, how it works in your body and brain, and how it can change you physically and mentally. It covers the risk factors, prevention, and treatment of meth abuse, too. You'll also read stories of people who've lived with addiction and had to overcome it.

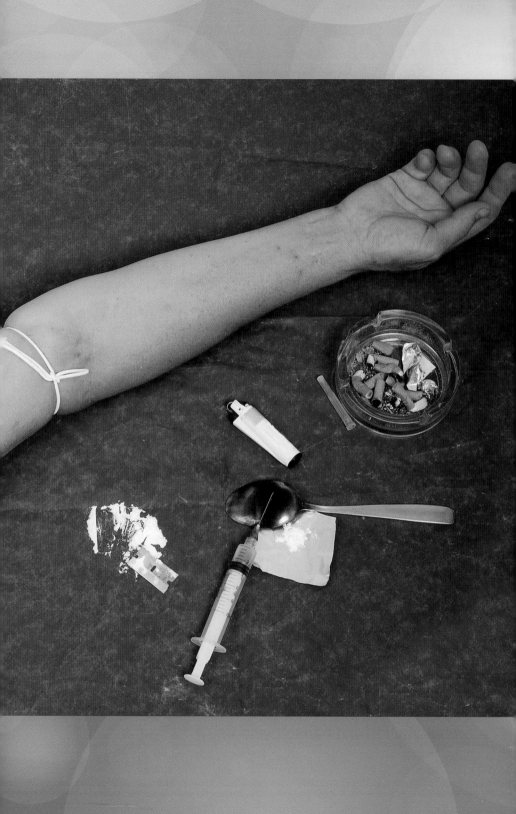

Chapter 1

THE "SPEED" Drug

Nic Sheff had everything going for him. He was smart, funny, got good grades in school, and had lots of friends. He loved movies, reading, writing, drawing, and surfing. Growing up in California with a writer for a dad, he met lots of interesting, even famous, people. His father, David, eventually wrote a bestselling book about Nic called *Beautiful Boy*.

The book was about Nic's addiction to marijuana and then methamphetamine. Nic's drug abuse started early. He got drunk for the first time at age eleven, during a family ski trip. His parents believed him when he said he threw up from food poisoning. A year later, David found marijuana in Nic's backpack. Nic promised never to try pot again, and his father believed him—again. Or maybe he just wanted to.

In ninth grade, Nic was suspended from school for buying pot outside the cafeteria. Finally, his parents admitted that Nic had a drug problem, but they still made excuses. After all, lots of kids try pot, right? Nic was going to a school counselor, was on the swim team, and was getting good grades. So his parents told themselves that his "experiment" with pot was over.

It wasn't. Nic later admitted, "When I was sixteen, I started smoking pot every day."[1]

Nic's drug use escalated after he graduated from high school. That summer, he disappeared for several days. But first, he stole money and wine from his parents. Frantic with worry, they called his friends, the police, and hospital emergency rooms. When Nic finally returned home, he was angry and hostile. Two weeks later, the police came to the house and led Nic away in handcuffs. He was supposed to have appeared in court for marijuana possession but hadn't shown up. He never told his parents about the charges. They bailed him out of jail and were sure the arrest had taught him a lesson.

No way. Nic went to college that fall and lasted only one semester. He came home more strung out than ever. He disappeared again for several days, and then called home begging for help. David found Nic behind trash cans in an alley. He was filthy, skinny, and his eyes looked black and empty. Nic collapsed into his father's arms, admitting, "I learned how dangerous meth is. I'm not stupid. I'll never mess with it again."[2]

David was stunned and horrified. Nic was doing meth? He begged his son to go into a drug treatment program, and Nic finally agreed. The staff at the treatment center said that Nic was taking so many different drugs he could easily have died.

During treatment, Nic confessed that after high school, "I took whatever I could find—ecstasy, LSD, mushrooms, and then . . . then crystal. When I tried it, I felt better than ever before in my life."[3]

It would be great if Nic's story of addiction ended here. If he had recovered, returned to college, and then lived a normal life. But that didn't happen. Nic went back to using meth and other drugs again and again. By the time he was twenty-five, he'd gone to five different treatment centers. Sometimes, he stayed off drugs for over a year. During sober times, he exercised, worked at various jobs, and started writing a book about his experiences. But then he'd run into an old friend who was using drugs or he'd break up with his girlfriend. Something stressful would happen in Nic's life to make him turn to drugs again.

Nic ended up homeless, sleeping in city parks or his car, begging for money, and eating from garbage cans. He stole money from his parents and his eight-year-old brother and forged checks. He stole needles and pain medicine from a friend's mother who had cancer. His arm became so infected from injecting drugs he almost had it amputated. He overdosed, was hooked up to life support, and nearly died.

Nic's parents lived in a state of constant fear. They were afraid to hear the phone ring, thinking it was bad news about Nic. They refused to give him money, but said they would pay for his treatment. His mom and dad had

expected Nic to go to college, get married, have children, and have a good job and a good life. In the end, they were just grateful he was still alive.

Nic eventually stayed drug-free long enough to finish his book, *Tweak: Growing Up on Methamphetamines*. It was published in 2008, the same time as David's book. Together, father and son made public appearances to talk about their books and how drug addiction had affected their lives.

Nic went back to drugs at least two more times after his book was published. But he quickly checked himself into treatment centers. Today, he is married, has written another book, and has been drug-free for several years. But he knows better than to get too confident. He learned the hard way that using drugs is a dangerous gamble, and that meth is one of the most addictive drugs. Here's what he said about his addiction:

"It's just this compulsion that I can't break. In that sense, I'll always be a drug addict. But I think I can be someone who no longer uses drugs."[4]

What Is Meth?

Methamphetamine (meth) is a white, odorless, bitter-tasting powder. It is also available in rock or "crystal" form, called crystal meth. The powder can be swallowed, inhaled through the nose (snorted), or mixed with water and injected through a needle. The crystal form is heated and smoked.

Some nicknames or "street" names for methamphet-amine are crystal, Christina, Tina, ice, glass, crank, chalk,

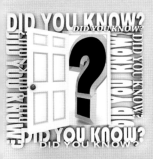
POWDER AND
Rock

Meth is sold
on the street in
several different
forms. Two
common forms
are powder
and rock, also
known as
crystal meth.

Illegal labs use several toxic ingredients to make illegal meth.

fire, go fast, geep, poor man's coke, and truck drivers. Someone who is addicted to meth is called a speed freak, tweaker, or meth head.

Meth isn't a plant, and it doesn't occur naturally. It's synthetic, meaning it's made in a lab by mixing several poisonous (toxic) substances and one legal drug. Many toxic ingredients, like drain cleaner or antifreeze, are used to make meth and are easy to buy. But the most important ingredients aren't. Meth can't be made without either ephedrine or pseudoephedrine. These ingredients are found in common household drugs, like cold, allergy, and asthma medicines and cough syrup. All of these medicines are sold in drugstores.

When the U.S. Food and Drug Administration found out people were using drugstore medicines to make illegal meth, they tightened up the laws. Since 2006, people have been required to sign their names, show identification, and only buy small amounts of these medicines at one time. Unfortunately, people who want to make meth badly enough find ways around these rules.

Most of the meth abused in this country is made in big laboratories called "super labs" in the United States and in Mexico. However, people also make meth for personal use in their houses, garages, and even in their cars.

The Brain-Changing Drug

Meth is one of the most addictive of all drugs. Experts say people can become hooked after trying it only once. This probably happened to Nic, who said the first time he took meth he felt "strong and confident, just like a superstar."[5]

So he kept using the drug again and again, trying to get those awesome feelings back. But he never could.

That's what happens with meth. It heads straight for the brain and produces a state of euphoria, also called a "high" or a "rush." But this feeling decreases the more a person uses meth. Why? Because over time, meth changes how the brain works by messing with a very important chemical called dopamine.

Dopamine is known as the "feel good" chemical because it allows people to feel pleasure. Dopamine is produced in the brain, and when people take meth, dopamine pours out of their brains. But then, meth destroys most of the dopamine. When the drug wears off, the person "crashes"—comes down from the high and feels depressed, exhausted, even suicidal. Meth causes a severe chemical imbalance in the brain. Even if a person stops using the drug, his brain may never recover completely.

Meth belongs to a class of drugs known as stimulants. It also belongs to a group of stimulant drugs called amphetamines. A stimulant speeds up the central nervous system and makes a person feel wide awake and energetic. That's why meth is nicknamed "speed." Stimulants also make the heart beat faster and decrease appetite. Coffee and nicotine are also stimulants. Coffee might keep you awake at night, but meth prevents users from sleeping for days. The drug is also known to cause violent behavior and frightening experiences of seeing, hearing, and feeling things that aren't real. It might even kill you.

Close-Up of a Nerve Cell in the Brain

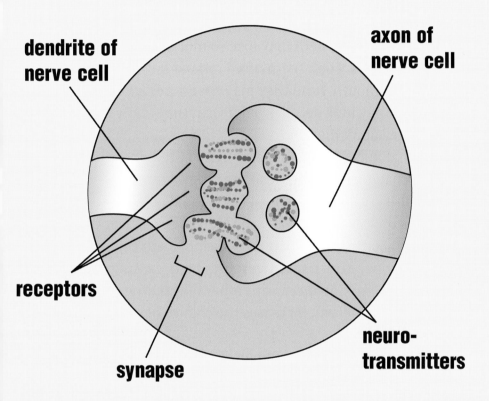

dendrite of nerve cell

axon of nerve cell

receptors

synapse

neuro-transmitters

The brain has many nerve cells, or neurons. The parts of a neuron, the axon and dendrite, "talk" to each other using neurotransmitters. When a neuron wants to talk to another neuron, it releases neurotransmitters from its axon. The neurotransmitters cross the synapse and attach to the dendrite of another neuron. When a person takes methamphetamine, or another drug, this process is interrupted and can cause the person to act in a different manner.

The Body-Snatching Drug

Meth doesn't just destroy the brain; it destroys the body, too. In most cases, taking meth for even a few months can turn a healthy person into a physical wreck. After a few years, people on meth may lose so much weight they look like skeletons. Their teeth often rot and fall out (known as "meth mouth") and they may have sores all over their bodies. They look decades older than they really are. That is, if they don't die first.

What kills people on meth? They're at risk for heart attacks and strokes, because the drug causes high blood pressure, irregular heartbeats, and rapid pulse. Meth also causes the heart lining and the blood vessels near the brain to become inflamed. In addition, meth can make body temperature rise dangerously high, causing coma and death. Mixing meth with other illegal drugs, like cocaine and heroin, increases the chance of overdose and sudden death.

Meth changes people's personalities, too, until they become like strangers to their families and friends. Like many drugs, meth can cause people to lie and steal from those they love. Even gentle, kind people may become aggressive, hostile, and dangerous. Meth also causes users to abandon their good judgment and do things they wouldn't normally do. This includes having unprotected sex and sharing needles. That's why many meth users contract HIV/AIDS or hepatitis C, diseases that can kill you. These diseases are other ways meth "snatches" a person's healthy body.

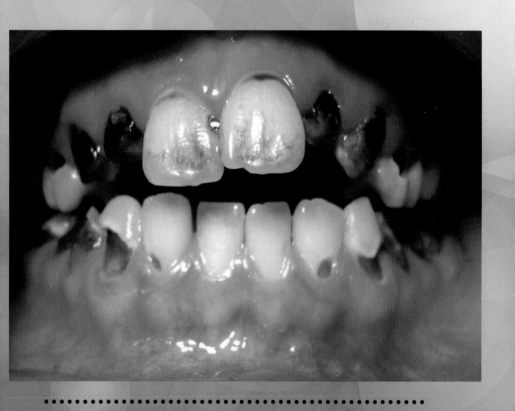

This is a case of suspected meth mouth, which causes the teeth to rot.

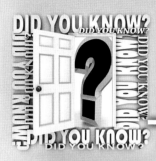

NOT ALL METH
Is Bad

Methamphetamine also has legal uses. It's sold by prescription under the trade name Desoxyn. Very low doses in pill or liquid form are used to treat ADHD, or attention deficit hyperactivity disorder. This disorder causes children and adults to have trouble concentrating and completing tasks. Taken properly, following doctor's orders, the drug helps people calm down and focus. But taken improperly, the prescription drug can cause many of the health problems associated with street methamphetamine.

Doctors also prescribe low doses of methamphetamine for narcolepsy, which causes people to become very drowsy and fall asleep at inconvenient times. The drug increases their alertness. Occasionally, the drug is also prescribed for weight loss, because it helps burn calories and makes people less hungry. But it's only used for severely overweight people when all other weight loss methods fail. In these cases, patients are closely supervised by their doctors to be sure they're taking the drug correctly.

Some Scary Statistics

According to *The Meth Epidemic*, a television documentary, 1.4 million Americans use meth illegally, and the number is rising. Around the world, there are 26 million meth addicts, as many as for heroin addicts and cocaine addicts combined.[6]

Meth is relatively cheap. One-fourth gram costs about $25. This is the size of a small paper clip. Because it's cheap, meth may appeal to teens or even preteens. One 2011 study reported that 0.8 percent of eighth graders, 1.4 percent of tenth graders, and 1.4 percent of twelfth graders had tried the drug.[7]

Impact of Meth

Meth doesn't just destroy the people who take it, it also destroys families. Nic Sheff's story is a good example of how the drug ruins trust and tears families apart. When the meth addict is a parent, young children are put in danger while the parent gets high, goes out to buy meth, or makes meth at home. Many children of meth addicts are taken away from parents and placed in foster care.

Meth destroys communities by making it dangerous to walk the streets or even stay in your own home. Many prison inmates are in jail for meth-related crimes, such as robbery, assault, identity theft, domestic violence, and child endangerment. When addicts or dealers make meth at home, these makeshift labs sometimes explode, killing innocent people.

The healthcare system is also strained because so many meth users overdose or have other problems and

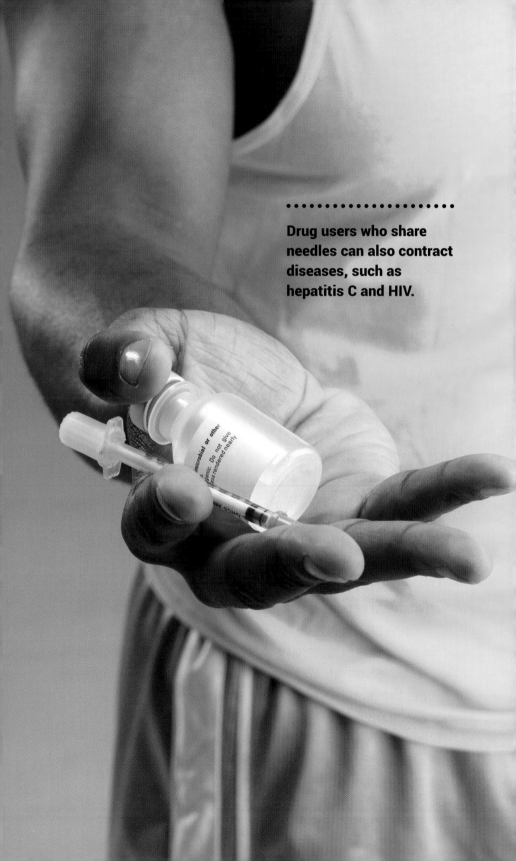

Drug users who share needles can also contract diseases, such as hepatitis C and HIV.

visit hospital emergency rooms. In 2009, the National Institute on Drug Abuse reported that 93,562 emergency room visits were due to abuse of meth and other stimulant drugs.[8] The number of deadly diseases, such as HIV/AIDS and hepatitis C, also rises with meth use and puts an added burden on the healthcare system.

Recovering from Meth

Sadly, there is no medicine that will cure meth addiction, although research is ongoing. Meth has the highest relapse rate of any addictive drug. Still, recovery is possible. It took Nic Sheff many years and many trips to rehab. And relapse is still a constant threat.

Even sadder, people who actually stop using meth may take a long time to recover. They often have memory loss and poor coordination because the nerves in their brains are damaged. Eventually, the brain may repair itself, but it can take years.

There's a saying in addiction recovery programs that "Once is too many and 1,000 is never enough." This is especially true for meth. The drug is so addictive, you can get hooked the first time you use it. After that, you can never get enough.

Chapter 2

A DRUG
Gone Wrong

The history of meth begins in China. The Chinese have practiced herbal medicine for over 5,000 years. One of the herbs they use is "ma huang", or ephedra. Records from 1,800 years ago show that doctors used ma huang to create a powder or tea. They used it to treat people with cold or flu symptoms, such as coughing, headaches, general body aches, and trouble breathing.

What does that have to do with meth? Fast forward to 1885. A Japanese doctor named Nagai isolated the part of the ephedra plant that made it so useful. He named this white, odorless powder ephedrine, a stimulant.

In 1887, a chemist in Germany synthesized the first amphetamine. To synthesize is to combine parts to make something new and more complex. The chemical structure of the new drug was a lot like that of ephedrine. In Japan in 1893, Nagai also synthesized a drug from ephedrine called methamphetamine. In 1919, crystal meth was first created. The new crystal powder could be dissolved in water, which meant it could be injected.

Confused? You aren't the only one. The chemical structure of meth and amphetamine is similar but not exactly alike. They are both stimulants like ephedrine. But meth, especially crystal meth, can be far more dangerous. For many years, people used both meth and amphetamine for the same purpose. That's why much of their history coincides.

Finding a Purpose for a Drug

For over thirty years no one could figure out how to use these drugs. At the beginning of the twentieth century, medicine based on science was a new idea. Drug companies still sold traditional herbs for healing. Adrenaline was one of the first new drugs marketed. Adrenaline occurs naturally in our bodies, but the drug form of adrenaline came from the glands of cows. It relaxed the tissues of the lungs and became a popular remedy for asthma. It also gave relief to people with stuffy noses.

During the 1920s, researchers discovered that ephedrine worked in the same way. Not surprising. The Chinese had been using it to relieve breathing problems for at least 5,000 years! Ephedrine became popular for people with asthma. It was in such demand that China couldn't grow enough ephedra to keep up with it. Scientists looked for an alternative.

Ephedra plants have been used for thousands of years as a remedy for breathing problems.

In 1927, Gordon Alles, a chemist in Los Angeles, synthesized his own version of amphetamine. He hoped to discover a new treatment for allergies and asthma. When Alles tested the drug on himself, he described a "feeling of well being" followed by a "rather sleepless night." He knew he had stumbled on something important.[1]

In 1932, a drug company named Smith, Kline & French (SKF) began selling over-the-counter amphetamine inhalers called Benzedrine for congestion. The company bought Alles's patent and, in 1937, began to market prescription amphetamine pills as Benzedrine. That same year, the American Medical Association (AMA) approved advertising Benzedrine for the treatment of narcolepsy, mild depression, and Parkinson's disease. Parkinson's is a brain disorder that leads to shaking and difficulty with body movement.

Studies soon showed that amphetamine had other benefits. It curbed people's appetites, making it a potential diet drug. It also calmed children who were hyperactive. Meth had the same benefits. Both drugs were beginning to find a purpose.

The War on Speed

Meth and amphetamine found their home during World War II. Studies showed that the drugs seemed to increase energy and alertness. In 1938, meth was sold to the German people in the form of a pill called Pervitan. By 1939, the German army discovered that meth also made soldiers more aggressive.

METHAMPHETAMINE

The chemical structures of methamphetamine and amphetamine are similar. Although they are both stimulants, meth can be much more dangerous.

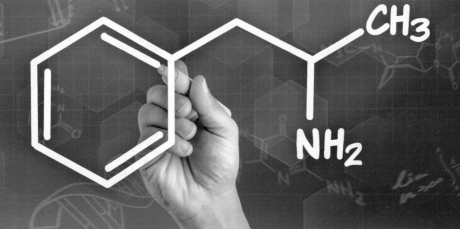
AMPHETAMINE

CH₃

NH₂

The German army discovered that meth made soldiers more aggressive. In this 1944 scene from a German film, a Nazi soldier carries ammunition boxes in territory taken by their counter-offensive.

For the Germans, the war was about speed and shock. They called their attack method *blitzkrieg*, which means "lightning war" in English. The Germans had the latest technology—the fastest tanks, the most accurate bombers, and meth. Their soldiers, pilots, and tank drivers seemed fearless. From September 1939 to June 1940, they rapidly conquered Poland, Denmark, Norway, Holland, Belgium, and France. History can only guess at the role meth played in their lightning war.

German doctors, though, had doubts about meth. Did it really improve a soldier's performance? Or did it just make him "feel" more confident? Evidence showed that overconfidence from meth caused some soldiers to make dangerous mistakes. The drug also had bad side effects. It made soldiers irritable and unable to control their aggression. Also, meth seemed to be addictive. It took too long for soldiers to get back to normal after taking it. By 1941, the German military was discouraging its use.

While the Germans were discouraging meth, the British military approved amphetamine use. The Americans did, too. They issued Benzedrine pills to help soldiers fight "combat fatigue." Pilots on long-range bombing missions used them to stay awake. The "feel good" characteristic of speed seemed to improve morale and create tougher soldiers. American and British soldiers using amphetamines had the same side effects as the German soldiers on meth. But the militaries of both countries ignored the problem.

No military used meth more effectively during the war than the Japanese. They distributed it to soldiers and

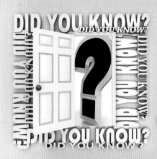

HITLER
on Meth?

From 1942 until his death in 1945, Adolp Hitler received daily injections of crystal meth from his doctor. Was Hitler being treated for Parkinson's disease, as some historians suggest? Or was the meth a remedy for depression and fatigue? Film from the period shows Hitler's body would sometimes shake on one side. If he did suffer from Parkinson's, the amounts of meth he took would have made it worse. There's no telling how the drug may have affected a man who was already violent and out of touch with reality.

factory workers alike. But Japanese kamikaze pilots took it to the limit. The pilots were usually young men ready to die for their emperor. Before leaving on suicide missions, they were injected with heavy doses of meth. Then they would crash their planes, loaded with explosives, into ships or other targets, destroying themselves and their targets in the process.

The Post-War Years

The Japanese made so much meth during the war they had a surplus afterward. Japanese drug companies sold the drug to the public. Its street name was "shabu", it resulted in an epidemic of meth abuse in Japan that continued into the 1950s.

The situation wasn't as bad in the United States—yet. Meth and amphetamine were still prescription drugs, but sales shot up. About 800 million tablets were sold in 1945. By 1962, the number reached about 8 billion, according to the Food and Drug Administration (FDA). Why? Drug companies began to compete with each other, flooding the market with amphetamine and meth. Some companies sold generic amphetamine. Others sold meth as Methedrine and Desoxyn. Prescriptions were easy to get and even available on the black market. Meanwhile demand from the public continued to rise:

◆ Diet doctors prescribed "uppers" for weight loss.

◆ College students took "pep pills" to study, and truck drivers used them to stay awake on the job.

◆ Homemakers took speed for mild depression, and athletes took it so they could perform better.

◆ The U.S. military gave amphetamine to the troops fighting the Korean War in the early 1950s.

The "feel good" quality of these drugs invited abuse from the time they appeared in the late 1930s. After the war, the abuse got worse. Inhalers were the big problem. The nasal strips inside were soaked with the equivalent

The U. S. military gave amphetamine to troops in Korea. Here, U.S. Marines move forward after effective air support flushed out the enemy from the hillside.

of a jar of meth or amphetamine pills. Inhalers weren't dangerous if used properly, but people would pull off the strips and swallow the drug to get high. Then they began to extract the drugs from the strips for injection. Worse yet, you could buy inhalers without a prescription. Artists, writers, jazz musicians, and ex-servicemen (who'd become addicted) were the worst abusers. In 1959, the FDA ruled that amphetamine inhalers could only be sold by prescription. Meth inhalers didn't require a prescription until 1965.

During the 1950s, the destructive effects of meth and amphetamine became obvious. Some people had been using the drugs for years, gradually increasing the amount they took. Long-time users were showing up in emergency rooms with symptoms of paranoid delusions. There were reports of a new mental disorder: "amphet-amine psychosis." Meth and amphetamine seemed to be the cause. After patients stopped taking the drugs, many recovered from their "psychosis" in a week or two.

The Rise of Meth Use

By the 1960s, new drugs began to replace amphetamine as an antidepressant. It was still popular for other uses—and abuses. People took it to control weight, to stay awake, and to increase athletic ability. Even President Kennedy was known to get injections of an amphetamine "cocktail" to boost his energy level.

During the 1960s, there was an increased demand for meth as a recreational drug. The West Coast of the United States was a hot spot. As demand increased, so did

Young women who dream of becoming "dancer slim" may make the mistake of resorting to use methamphetamine to lose weight.

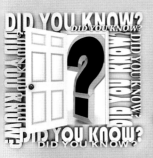

A PERFORMANCE-ENHANCING Drug

During the 1950s and 60s, meth and amphetamine caught on with athletes as a way to improve performance. The drugs were soon banned in high school and college sports. Professional athletes continued to use them in sports such as cycling, football, baseball, and ice hockey. But at what risk? At the 1960 Olympics, Knut Jensen, a Danish cyclist, died of a heart attack after collapsing in a race. Tom Simpson lost consciousness while racing in the 1967 Tour de France and died from heart failure later that day. He was only 29 years old. Both athletes had amphetamines in their system.

Some athletes use amphetamine today, even though the drug is banned by most sports organizations. Gymnasts, ballet dancers, and wrestlers use it to reduce body weight. Others take it to build muscle, improve endurance, and recover from injuries faster. The drug may increase self confidence, but it distorts a person's view of reality. Athletes have been known to play when they're injured, without realizing it, often ending their careers. Using the drug during strenuous physical activity increases an athlete's heart rate and body temperature, which can be life-threatening.

addictions. More people injected meth instead of taking pills. Home labs that manufactured meth for personal use appeared. Super labs produced meth for the streets. Compulsive drug users were called "speed freaks." Their behavior was violent and unpredictable. "Speed Kills" was a popular slogan.

The government began to crack down on the illegal use of meth and amphetamine. In 1970, Congress passed the Controlled Substance Act. It authorized the Drug Enforcement Administration (DEA) to classify all forms of amphetamine as Schedule II drugs. A Schedule II drug has a medical use but a high potential for abuse. It may lead to physical or psychological dependence and is only available by prescription. The government also began to educate people about the dangers of meth and amphetamine.

By the mid-1980s, the number of prescriptions written for amphetamine pills dropped 90 percent.[2] Drug companies were the best source of amphetamine, so it was less available on the street. But meth was another story. It was easy to make and illegal production took off. Outlaw biker gangs in California and the Pacific Northwest cornered the market on speed.

A Different Kind of Drug

The government had a dilemma on its hands. Meth was different from other drugs. It wasn't being smuggled into the country. It was made here with ingredients that were legal. Those ingredients were also widely available to the public at large . One of these ingredients was given the

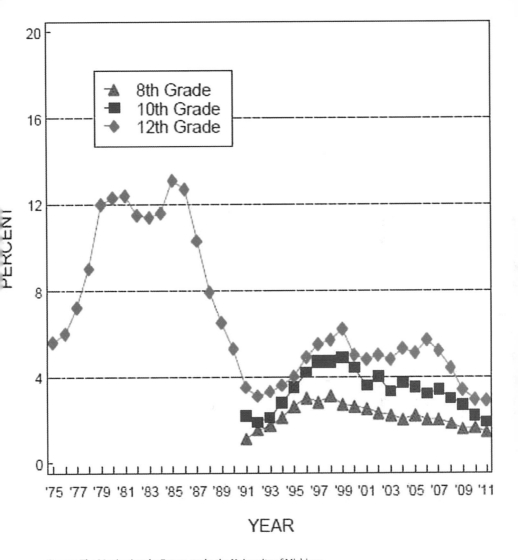

Source: The Monitoring the Future study, the University of Michigan.

This chart shows the percent of students who used illegal drugs between 1975 and 2011.

President John F. Kennedy used injections of amphetamines to boost his energy level.

name P2P or phenyl-2-propanone. In 1980, the federal government put strict controls on the use of P2P.

That didn't stop the meth labs. They used ephedrine instead. It made a purer form of meth—crystal meth. It was twice as powerful and twice as dangerous. A Mexican drug cartel began supplying ephedrine to the bikers' meth labs. A drug cartel is an illegal organization that controls the production and distribution of narcotics. To make matters worse, an even purer form of meth that could be smoked was introduced. It was called "ice."

In 1988, the DEA began to regulate the sale of chemicals used to make meth. The list included ephedrine and pseudoephedrine, another chemical found in ephedra. The drug industry fought back. They used both chemicals in over-the-counter cold pills. The DEA gave in. They agreed to regulate the raw materials used, not the pills themselves. Soon meth labs were buying cold pills and extracting the needed chemicals from them.

The new regulations drove the labs further underground. Meth's use spread slowly to the Midwest and the South. Rural areas were an ideal place to make meth. It was easy to hide in a remote area, and the needed chemical supplies were more readily available. Law enforcement in these areas was spread thin. Also, meth was inexpensive. People in rural communities could afford it.

During the 1990s, the Mexican cartel bought ephedrine from factories overseas and smuggled it into the U.S. They were the same factories that provided ephedrine to the drug companies for cold medicines! An explosion of meth labs, meth use, and meth addiction followed. The United

States asked foreign manufacturers not to sell to the cartel. They agreed and ephedrine became scarce for a time. But a new source of pseudoephedrine was found in Canada where the chemical wasn't regulated yet.

By 2003, a National Survey on Drug Use and Health estimated that 12 million Americans over the age of 12 had tried meth. That same year, Canada cracked down on exports of pseudoephedrine. But in 2004, Mexico imported a large supply for cold pills. Almost half was cooked into meth and smuggled into the United States.

In 2005, Congress passed the Combat Methamphetamine Epidemic Act. It required store owners to keep products with pseudoephedrine under lock and key. Buyers had to register at the store counter in order to

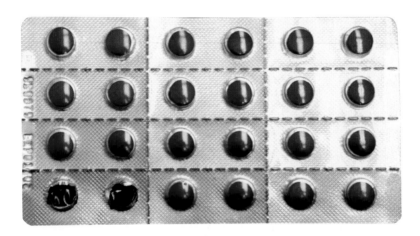

Pseudoephedrine is a chemical found in cold medications sold over the counter at many pharmacies. Pseudoephedrine is sometimes used to make methamphetamine.

Methamphetamine became known as a biker drug because of its popularity with motorcycle gangs on the West Coast.

purchase them. Since then, several states have considered making them prescription-only medications. In 2011, legislation was introduced to make pseudoephedrine a prescription drug nationwide. So far, the drug industry has lobbied successfully to interfere with that effort.

America's Speed Habit

Meth and amphetamine are still used today to treat children with Attention Deficit Hyperactivity Disorder (ADHD). In the 1960s, a diagnosis of ADHD was rare. By the early 2000s, between four and five million people

were diagnosed with the disorder, including adults. Some experts question how many really need the drugs.

The military still allows amphetamine use during war, in spite of its troubling side effects. In 2002, U.S. pilots in Afghanistan killed and wounded Canadian soldiers in "friendly fire." The pilots had taken amphetamine, which may have affected their judgment.

Today, meth is more potent and dangerous than in the past. Most users smoke it or inject it. Meth and amphetamine were once drugs of hope. Today, that hope is debatable.

Chapter 3

DANGER:
Speed Trap!

On November 18, 2013, sixteen-year-old Cruz Marcelino Velazquez was attempting to walk across the border from Tijuana, Mexico, to San Diego, California. Border officers noticed the teen was acting nervous. They became more suspicious when they discovered he was carrying two small containers of amber-colored liquid.

When questioned, Cruz claimed the liquid was apple juice. The officers took him to an inspection office, where the teen attempted to persuade them the liquid was apple juice by drinking a big swallow of it. Afterwards, he began screaming in pain, said something about "the chemicals," and then shouted, "My heart, my heart!" in Spanish.[1]

Cruz was taken to a nearby hospital and died about two hours later. The medical examiner's report showed the cause of death was acute methamphetamine intoxication.

Joe Garcia, assistant special agent in charge of U.S. Immigration and Customs Enforcement Investigations in San Diego, said there has been an "alarming increase" in the number of children caught with methamphetamine at the San Diego border crossing.[2] Children are typically paid $50 to $200 a trip.

To avoid detection when crossing borders, people dissolve crystal meth in water and put it in juice bottles, windshield wiper fluid containers, and gas tanks. Experts say the liquid is a very pure form of meth that is used to produce the more common powder form of the drug. Because the liquid is so pure, drinking even small amounts can be deadly.

According to his high school principal, Cruz was an average student with no discipline problems who regularly attended classes. He also had no previous criminal record.[3]

The medical examiner's report doesn't indicate that the inspectors asked the boy to drink the liquid or if they had a chance to stop him when he volunteered.

What Is Addiction?

A wise person once said, "Insanity is repeating the same mistakes and expecting different results." This quote, probably from a Narcotics Anonymous booklet, is often used to describe how an addict thinks—or doesn't think. People who are addicted to drugs like meth know deep down that the drug is bad for them and will make their lives worse. But they still take the drug over and over again, expecting their lives to miraculously get better.

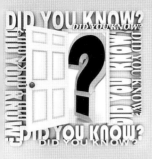

WHAT IS "Tweaking"?

"Tweaking" describes the uncontrollable, repetitive behaviors of meth users. Examples of tweaking include:

◆ Picking at the skin until it bleeds and scabs

◆ Rocking or making jerky, twitchy body movements

◆ Clenching the jaw or grinding the teeth

◆ Combing or brushing the hair for hours

◆ Housecleaning compulsively

◆ Drawing the same thing over and over

◆ Playing a video game repeatedly

◆ Crawling on the carpet looking for dropped meth

◆ Shopping or gambling online compulsively

◆ Taking things apart, like computers, and not putting them back together

Tweaking also refers to the way someone acts after they've taken meth for several days straight (a binge). They usually haven't eaten or slept for days. This causes them to see and hear things that aren't there (hallucinate). They may also hurt themselves or attack other people.

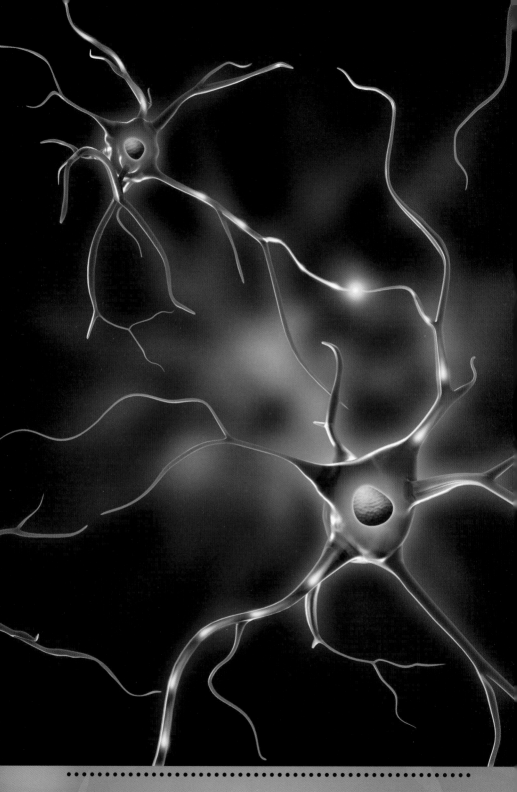

Neurons communicate with each other by sending neurotransmitters across a synapse to the next nerve cell.

Addiction is defined as a brain disease that causes people to become uncontrollably dependent on a substance or behavior. Some experts divide addiction into two types: substance and process. Substance addiction includes being hooked on things like drugs, alcohol, or smoking. Process addiction includes being hooked on activities like gambling or shopping. Research shows that addictions overlap. For example, people might abuse both drugs and alcohol and also gamble or shop compulsively.

A person with an addiction is called an addict. One common trait in addicts is refusing to admit they have a problem. This is called denial. It often takes a crisis—like going to jail or almost dying—to make people face up to their addiction.

How the Brain Rewards Us

All addictive drugs, including meth, affect the reward pathway in the center of brain. This pathway contains millions of nerve cells and controls motivation, behavior, and pleasure. Its main job is to make people feel good when they eat, drink, have sex, or do other behaviors that ensure their survival or the survival of the species.

Let's say you're eating a juicy hamburger. Yum! Your five senses tell your brain you're munching on something good. This message travels to the nerves in the reward pathway, triggering the release of the chemical dopamine, which is stored in the brain's nerve cells. Dopamine pours out of the nerve cells and floats around in the open spaces between nerve endings. These spaces are called synapses.

Across the synapses, in the receiving nerve cells, dopamine receptors are ready and waiting. These receptors are like electrical sockets. Only dopamine, or a substance almost identical to it, can plug into these sockets. When dopamine plugs in, we feel pleasure. But pleasure doesn't last forever, so after a while, the dopamine is shipped back to the sending nerve cells to be used later. Excess dopamine is destroyed.

Dopamine is called the feel-good chemical because it causes a little jolt of pleasure. That feeling of pleasure is your reward for eating the hamburger and nourishing your body.

Why do you need a reward? Because if you didn't feel that pleasurable jolt, food would be tasteless and you'd probably skip eating. The same goes for sex. If it didn't feel good, no one would bother doing it and the human species would die out. The reward pathway makes us repeat feel-good behaviors by connecting to parts of the brain that control memory and behavior. It tells the brain, "Hey, pay attention. This is important. Remember it."

Meth on the Brain

Drugs—even legal ones—are chemicals. They all have an effect on the brain. Drugs of abuse, like nicotine, marijuana, and meth, affect the brain's reward system in varying degrees.

What happens when meth enters the brain? Total chaos! When it reaches the brain, it causes a tsunami of dopamine to flood out of the nerve cells. Who needs the five senses? It bypasses them, slamming into the brain's reward circuitry and causing intense pleasure and exhilaration. The nerve

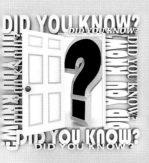

WAYS TO
Take Meth

There are four ways to take meth: smoking, injecting, inhaling, or eating. People who smoke meth generally use a glass pipe. They heat pieces of crystal meth in the pipe, which turns the meth into a liquid, and inhale the vapors. Smoking produces an intense rush in only five to ten seconds.

People who inject meth with a needle must first dissolve the powdered drug in water. This route also produces an intense rush in only five to ten seconds.

Inhaling powdered meth produces a rush in three to five minutes. Eating powdered meth is the least popular way to take it, because the rush doesn't occur for fifteen to twenty minutes. People mix it in a drink, put it on a knife and eat it, fill a capsule with it and take it like a pill, or even wrap it in toilet paper and swallow it.

Crystal meth, or ice, is a pure form of methamphetamine that can be smoked. It looks like ice chips and is smoked using a glass pipe like the one shown in this picture.

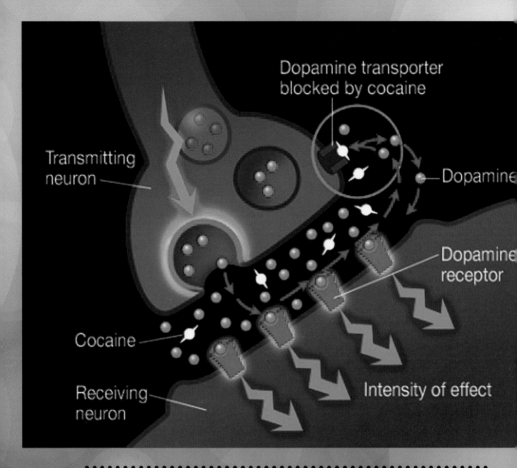

In the normal communication process, dopamine is released by a neuron into the synapse, where it can bind to dopamine receptors on neighboring neurons. Normally, dopamine is then recycled back into the transmitting neuron by a specialized protein called the dopamine transporter. If meth is present, it attaches to the dopamine transporter and blocks the normal recycling process, resulting in a buildup of dopamine in the synapse, which contributes to the pleasurable effects of meth.

cells get overstimulated and dopamine keeps pouring out, causing a high that lasts up to twelve hours!

To make matters worse, meth is tricky. Its chemical composition is a lot like dopamine's, so the brain thinks it is dopamine. The brain gets mixed up and ships the meth back to the sending nerve cells, while the real dopamine gets left behind, floating around in the synapses. Now totally confused, the brain destroys the real dopamine and stores the meth in the cells.

Eventually, if a person keeps taking meth, the amount of dopamine in the brain gets almost used up. It takes more and more meth to feel good. Eventually, there isn't enough dopamine to make a person very high anymore, or even to create a feeling of pleasure. At this point, meth users crash. They feel exhausted, hungry, depressed, or maybe even suicidal.

In lab experiments with animals, meth caused dopamine levels in the brain to increase from 100 units to 1,250 units. That's twelve times the amount of dopamine that people get from naturally pleasurable activities, like food or sex.[4] This kind of high isn't normal, and the brain can't handle it. So it tries to adapt by reducing the number of dopamine receptors. As a result, the meth user will need more of the drug to get high. This is called tolerance to the drug.

Signs of Meth Use and Addiction

How can you tell if someone is using meth? The signs differ, depending on how long the person has been using

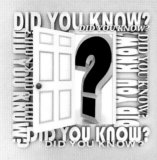

STAGES OF A *Meth High*

1. **Anticipation**: People get excited just thinking about the high.
2. **Administration**: The high occurs fastest with smoking and injecting. Snorting is third, and eating takes the longest.
3. **Initial rush**: Meth hits the brain and causes a chemical reaction, like a current of electricity. The heart races and blood pressure and pulse go wild. This intense rush lasts up to thirty minutes.
4. **High**: A total sense of well-being occurs for up to sixteen hours, but it isn't as intense as the initial rush. The user feels smart, confident, even superhuman. People may focus on a meaningless task, such as cleaning the same window over and over or taking their computer apart.
5. **Indecisiveness**: This stage lasts another six to ten hours. Users wonder if they should do more meth or crash.
6. **Binge**: If the user takes more meth to avoid crashing, this is a binge. It can last up to a couple weeks. Each time the person takes meth, he gets a weaker and weaker rush. During a binge, people become hyperactive and rarely sleep.
7. **Tweaking**: This occurs at the end of a binge, when the meth no longer makes a person high. The user feels empty and craves the drug. He may hallucinate and may hurt himself or others.
8. **Crash**: If more meth isn't taken, the body goes into protection mode. People sleep for one to three days, which lets their brain and body recover somewhat.
9. **Meth hangover**: People wake up mentally and physically exhausted, starved, and dehydrated. This stage lasts up to fourteen days. If they aren't in rehab, addicts usually return to using meth to "cure" themselves.
10. **Withdrawal**: If they don't take more meth, users go through withdrawal. Meth speeds you up and makes you high, and withdrawal is just the opposite. Users sleep for days, get depressed, have no energy, feel no pleasure, crave the drug, and often think of suicide. Withdrawal can last up to ninety days.

Tweaking behavior might include taking things apart, like computers, and not putting them back together.

• •

the drug. Here are some common signs of early, continued, and advanced meth use, as well as overdose:

Early meth use: Euphoria, nonstop talking, increased physical activity, lack of appetite, rapid eye movements, sweating, nervousness, shaky hands.

Continued meth use: Weight loss, shadows under eyes, pale complexion, acne or sores on skin, skin picking, strong body odor (from chemicals used to make meth), poor personal hygiene, aggressive or violent behavior, nail biting, nosebleeds, and depression.

Advanced meth use: Severe weight loss; hair loss; rotten or missing teeth; and symptoms of mental illness including hallucinations, panic, anger, repetitive behavior, and imagining people are out to get you (paranoia).

Overdose: Chest pain, high fever, fast breathing, sudden spike in blood pressure, severe sweating, confusion, convulsions, spike in body temperature. These problems can lead to heart attack, stroke, or coma.

Meth can kill you the first time you take it. Or it can kill you slowly over months and years. How much meth is a lethal dose? That depends on the person's body weight, what other drugs he or she is taking, what other medical problems are present, the strength of the meth, and the person's tolerance for the drug. Experts generally agree that an overdose can occur at relatively low levels, around 50 milligrams of pure meth in a non-tolerant user.[5] In other words, just a fraction of an ounce!

There is no "safe" amount of meth.

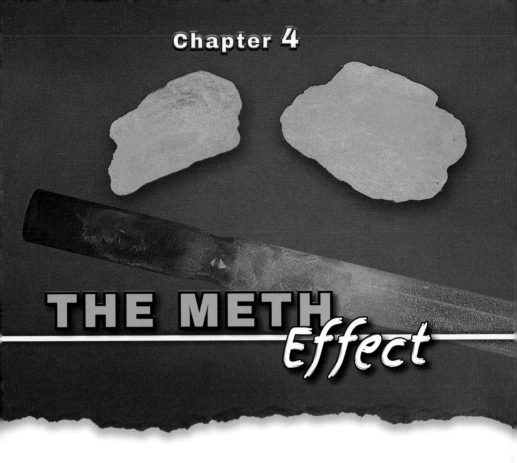

Chapter 4

THE METH Effect

Kim Wollenburg didn't think she was a meth addict. Never mind that she'd been smoking meth all day, every day for the past five years. Or that she'd been dealing meth almost as long. Hey, she owned a house, paid her bills, and took care of her son, Andy. She also didn't have rotten teeth or sores on her face like a lot of her customers. And she could stop any time she wanted to.

This is what she told herself until she hit rock bottom at age thirty-eight. She was facing three to five years in prison for felony possession with intent to distribute.

Flash back to Kim's younger days. She started using drugs at age twelve, progressing from alcohol to amphetamines, to pot, to acid. She stayed clean for a few years, but at age twenty-six, she started snorting cocaine daily.

Heavy methamphetamine users often say they see bugs crawling all over their skin.

Then she switched to crank—an impure form of meth. When her dealers moved away, she stayed clean for four years.

By all appearances, Kim was an overachiever. She was a single mother, raising a son with intellectual disabilities who had Down syndrome. Even so, Kim managed to hold down a job and attend college. For a few years, she even took care of foster children!

"I made sure I had plenty of mayhem going on around me, all in an effort to avoid the way I felt on the inside," Kim remembered.[1]

How she felt on the inside was worthless, ugly, and unloved.

Kim went back to college in her late twenties, and when exam time came, she was exhausted. She wanted something to help her study, so her brother got her some crank. For the next week, she snorted it every day, slept very little, studied all night, and aced all her finals.

When she ran out of crank, she crashed and wanted to sleep all the time. So she called her brother again. This time, he gave her meth. "I was addicted to meth the first time I tried it. Meth made me feel like I'd found what I'd been searching for all my life," Kim said.[2]

Soon, Kim started selling meth. She told herself it was okay because she could buy more things for Andy.

One side effect of smoking and selling meth was that Kim was late for everything all the time, including her "real" job. So she got fired. After Kim lost another job, she was forced to move in with her parents. She didn't get along with them, so she left Andy there and lived in her

Methamphetamine is sometimes smuggled into the country hidden in windshield wiper fluid bottles.

van for two months. Kim was a good liar, and her parents still didn't realize what she was doing.

During the next few years, Kim continued using and selling meth. She moved in with her boyfriend and ended up paying all his bills for three years. She found another addiction—playing poker online. She lost hundreds of thousands of dollars.

Kim was like a hamster on a treadmill. She couldn't give up the drug life or her boyfriend. She couldn't seem to get high enough anymore, even though she smoked huge amounts of meth. It wasn't fun or pleasurable. She just needed the drug to get through the day so she wouldn't fall apart.

One day, a meth dealer who'd become a police informant turned Kim in. She spent twenty-four hours in jail. After that, she went to an inpatient rehab center for thirty days. But once she returned home, it only took her twenty minutes to start smoking meth again. She still wasn't ready to quit.

Kim got off easy—the judge sentenced her to seven years' probation. But she stayed high, even when she went for the weekly urine tests for drugs. She tested positive for meth three times in a row. That's when the judge told her to clean up her act or go to prison.

Faced with a prison term and with the possibility of losing custody of her son, Kim finally admitted she was a meth addict. She went to a five-day hospital detox program and got clean for good on February 13, 2007, Andy's eighteenth birthday.

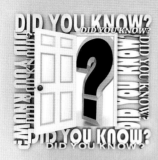

FACES of Meth

In 2004, Deputy Bret King of the Multnomah County, Oregon, Sheriff's Office, created the Faces of Meth project to show how meth use changes the way people look. He sorted through mug shots for people who had been arrested more than once for meth-related crimes. Then he put the photos next to each other to show how meth had ravaged the addicts' faces over the months and years.

King also started interviewing people in custody, asking about their meth experiences and what they would tell young people about the drug's dangers.

Since then, King has traveled to hundreds of class-rooms giving presentations and showing the mug shots. He tells kids, "I hope that in seeing this, you will make choices to not use methamphetamine, and that I will never see you come inside my jail."[3]

Today, Kim works for herself, selling custom-designed sugar cookies. She's been clean for six years and her business was featured in *Woman's Day* magazine in 2012.

"How do I stay sober? I respect my addiction," Kim said. "I make it a conscious decision every day."[4]

Meth's Toll on the Body

Meth can make a person look like a zombie in just a few months. Here are some ways the drug destroys a person's body, both inside and out:

Skin: Users imagine that insects (meth bugs) are crawling under their skin and try to pick them out. This causes open sores and permanent scars.

Teeth: Lack of brushing, bacteria, and grinding teeth together cause them to decay and fall out (meth mouth).

Hair: Poor nutrition and the poisonous chemicals in meth cause hair to fall out. Users may also compulsively pluck out their hair.

Muscles and bones: People on meth aren't hungry, so they get thin and frail. They lose muscle tone and their bones become brittle. Muscles in the body and face may twitch uncontrollably.

Body temperature: Meth can cause body temperature to rise way above 98.6 degrees. This is called hyper-thermia. High temperatures can cause brain damage, failure of the heart and other organs, coma, and even death.

Heart: Meth makes the heart beat harder, faster, and out of rhythm. Veins and arteries narrow, so less blood

gets through. This results in high blood pressure and, possibly, heart attack or stroke.

Lungs: Poisonous ingredients used to make meth can plug up blood vessels in the lungs. This can permanently decrease the amount of air the lungs take in.

Stomach and digestion: Meth slows digestion, so people aren't hungry or thirsty. They suffer from constipation, diarrhea, malnutrition, severe weight loss, dehydration, and stomach cramps.

Sex life: At first, meth increases sex drive. The drug also makes people do reckless things, like have unprotected sex. This puts them at risk for sexually transmitted diseases, like HIV/AIDS and hepatitis C. Before long, men who use meth may be unable to get an erection. Both women and men often lose interest in sex altogether. All they care about is using meth.

As Kim Wollenburg said, "You start out wanting to get high, and you end up needing not to come down."[5]

Meth's Effect on Pregnancy

Meth takes a terrible toll on the user's body. But when a pregnant woman takes the drug, it can have deadly consequences for her baby, too. High blood pressure can cause strokes in women and death in unborn babies. Women are also at risk for a rare, possibly fatal condition where the placenta separates from the uterus. This causes severe bleeding in the mother and lack of oxygen and possible brain damage in the baby. Women on meth also have a high risk of miscarriage—delivering too early for the baby to survive.

High blood pressure is a result of meth use.

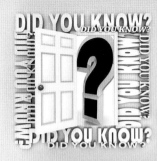

THE OTHER FACES
of Meth

Not all meth addicts look wasted; at least, not right away. And not all meth addicts are homeless and jobless. Some addicts and dealers might even be respected people in the community. Meth attracts many successful people because it makes them feel good and helps them lose weight. Here are some examples of the other faces of meth:

- **Michael Knibb, a bank vice president, was arrested in 2006 for having a crystal meth lab in his New York City penthouse.**

- **John Acerra, a middle-school principal in Bethlehem, Pennsylvania, was arrested in 2007 for selling crystal meth to police informants.**

- **Linda Clark, a sixty-year-old grandmother from Arkansas, was arrested in 2012 for buying quantities of pseudoephedrine tablets and selling them at a large profit to meth cooks.**

- **Monsignor Kevin Wallin, a Catholic priest in Bridgeport, Connecticut, was arrested in 2013 for possession with intent to distribute crystal meth.**

Experts agree that babies of meth users get less oxygen, so they're smaller than normal at birth. This means they often have problems with breathing, hearing, vision, and learning for the rest of their lives. Toddlers may also lag behind on tasks requiring fine motor skills, such as grasping objects.

Babies of meth users may also be born addicted to meth and have withdrawal symptoms. These include eating and sleeping problems, extreme irritability, trembling, and muscle spasms. If the mother has HIV/AIDS or hepatitis C, the baby probably also has it.

An ongoing study by the National Institute of Drug Abuse found that babies exposed to meth before birth have emotional and behavioral problems as they get older. The two hundred children studied were found to have more anxiety, depression, and emotional outbursts than normal children between ages three and five. Five-year-olds had trouble paying attention and were more destructive and aggressive than normal.[6]

The fact is, if babies are born with problems, many issues must be taken into account besides the mother's meth use. For example, was the pregnant woman smoking, drinking alcohol, or taking other drugs besides meth? Did she get good medical care while pregnant? Did she eat properly? Did she have a sexually transmitted disease?

Women on meth often take several drugs. They don't generally go to doctors, eat right, sleep enough, or take care of their health. They also neglect their children and expose them to dangerous living conditions. Chances are,

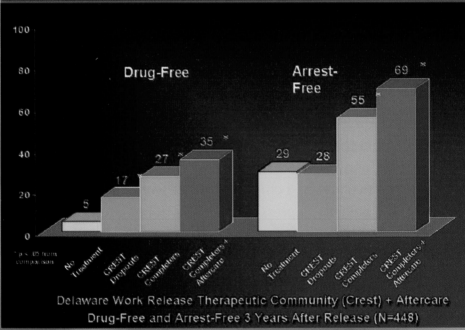

Source: Monitoring the Future.org

if an infant or child has problems, exposure to meth before birth is only one of many causes.

No one knows for sure how many pregnant women take meth. Unfortunately, we do know that meth use by pregnant teens appears to be rising. A recent government report studied girls ages thirteen to eighteen who were pregnant when they started treatment for drug abuse. They were asked what their main drug was. In 1992, 4.3 percent said meth. In 2007, 18.8 percent said meth.[7]

Meth Labs: Recipe for Ruin

Most people who use meth don't cook it themselves. Eighty percent of the meth in the United States comes from "super labs" in Mexico and the United States.[8] These labs are run by drug cartels. The other 20 percent of meth comes from small labs, usually in rural areas of the United States. People also cook small batches of meth just for themselves.

The super labs produce tons of meth in an assembly-line process, like in a factory. The process takes about two days and can create hundreds of thousands of doses of meth. Millions of dollars can be made off a two-day cook.

Meth made in Mexico is smuggled into the United States. It is often taped underneath tractor trailers, hidden inside packages of fruit or vegetables, or dissolved in water, beer, or windshield wiper fluid.

There are tens of thousands of small meth labs in the United States. Every state has people making the drug in their homes, barns, or garages. People use whatever equipment they can find and usually produce no more

than a few hundred doses. This is enough for their personal use and a few local sales.

The smallest labs of all are held in a person's hand. This method, called "shake and bake," involves putting the ingredients in a 2-liter plastic soda bottle and then heating it. Meth can be made in minutes, not hours, and the ingredients can be carried in a backpack and mixed in a bathroom stall or a car.

This method is extremely dangerous, because the ingredients are highly flammable. Removing the cap too soon or puncturing the bottle can cause an explosion. People have been seriously burned, blinded, or even killed trying to make meth this way.

What's in Meth?

Except for ephedrine or pseudoephedrine, the ingredients used to make meth are easy to find and not very expensive. Most of them are also highly poisonous. Would you inject drain cleaner into your arm? How about pouring antifreeze on your ice cream? These are two common ingredients used in cooking meth. A few others are red phosphorus (from match heads), ammonia, battery acid, iodine, and paint thinner.

When people cook meth, the inhaled ingredients can cause headaches, nausea, dizziness, skin irritation, and burns. The fumes are especially dangerous when meth is made in people's houses. Adults, innocent children, and pets suffer health problems. Sometimes the houses burn down. Meth contaminates the soil and water when the waste products are disposed of. Many smaller meth labs are planted in nice neighborhoods to avoid suspicion and are discovered when neighbors report strange odors to the police.

Legal Penalties for Meth

Possessing, selling, and making meth is illegal in all fifty states. Penalties range from paying a fine for possessing a small amount of meth to life in prison for selling or making meth. Generally, the more meth involved, the stiffer the penalty.

Besides jail time, people may have to pay thousands of dollars in fines and turn over any profits they made from the sale of meth. People who make meth may also have to pay for disposing of the drug and cleaning up the environment.

Going to jail is hitting rock bottom for some users. Others hit rock bottom when they lose everything—their homes, jobs, friends, families, health, good looks, and self-respect.

One addict said: "Imagine ten times worse than that. That's usually where rock bottom resides. And that's almost always where meth takes you."[9]

SAYING "NO" to Meth

The first time Alyssa* smoked marijuana, she was only thirteen. She wanted to get away from it all. School was a problem, her grades were poor, and people made fun of her. Weed made her feel happy. She loved it and smoked it several times a day. She even went to school high and skipped classes to smoke weed.

Alyssa had reason to be unhappy. Her mother was a meth addict who left when she was only three. Her oldest brother was in prison because of his meth use. Even some of her dad's old girlfriends had used it. But her older brother Kevin was clean. He didn't even smoke cigarettes. One day, Alyssa convinced Kevin to get stoned on marijuana. Pretty soon, they were both getting high on a regular basis.

*Not her real name

When Kevin started using meth a couple years later, Alyssa flipped out. Didn't he realize that meth had destroyed their family? She blamed herself for Kevin's drug use and begged him to stop.

Kevin went into rehab six months later and Alyssa wondered why everyone chose meth over her. She decided to try it.

Alyssa had seen what meth could do to people. They lost weight, their teeth rotted, and they seemed to be angry all the time. She was different, stronger. None of that would happen to her.

When Alyssa first got high, all she could think about was how good it felt. She wasn't as strong as she thought she was, though. Meth rapidly took over Alyssa's life. She used it every day. If she wasn't using, she felt depressed. She stopped eating and taking care of herself. She no longer did what she loved to do: singing, writing, playing sports. She got into fights with other people and swapped her true friends for other kids who got high. One day, she found herself sitting in the middle of the school football field. She suddenly realized that other students were watching her. Then it hit her. Alyssa was talking to people who weren't there.

Alyssa tried to hide her drug use, especially from her dad. She rarely went to school and made up friends so he wouldn't suspect. Nine months after Alyssa started using meth, she overdosed. Someone saw her hallucinating in the middle of the street and called the police. She ended up in the hospital. She had done so much damage to her body that she needed to learn to walk again.

Depression is one reason some people begin to use meth.

Afterwards, Alyssa spent three months in rehab where she alternated between wanting to get clean and wanting to call her drug friends to get her out. Alyssa's dad realized she needed more help and sent her to a rehab she couldn't leave. Alyssa's activities were strictly monitored. She missed her father and tried hard not to mess up so she could go home. She often stayed awake at night, crying. When the other girls talked about good times in their lives, Alyssa felt she had nothing to say. She realized how many good times she'd missed because she'd been high.

After a year in rehab, Alyssa was told she could go home. She moved into a group home with five other girls, some of them with drug addictions like hers. Alyssa enjoyed her new friends and went back to one of her old interests, writing. She worked on the school newspaper and became president of the student government. She also enjoyed spending time with her dad. Alyssa felt she had a purpose in life again.

Of course, Alyssa had to make changes in her life. She got rid of her old drug friends and avoided the places they hung out. When she felt like getting high, she said to herself, "Get that thought out of your head."[1]

Alyssa knows a part of her will always like drugs. But then she reminds herself about the consequences of using. She has been clean for over two years. Getting off meth wasn't easy and she wants to stay clean. Her life is better now that she's sober, and she doesn't want to throw it away.[2]

Falling into the Meth Trap

From early adolescence until the mid-twenties, a person's brain is a work in progress. The ability to reason and control impulses isn't fully developed. That's why teens have trouble controlling their emotions. That's also why they sometimes don't use good judgment or consider the negative consequences of using drugs or alcohol. More than any other age group, they are most at risk for permanent emotional or intellectual damage because of drugs.

Why do teens like Alyssa use crystal meth? For starters, she had problems she didn't want to face. Marijuana had shown her that drugs could make her forget her problems. Like many teens, she was also curious. Why had her mother and brothers chosen meth over her? What was so special about it? Even though Alyssa had seen the negative side effects of meth, she was sure that trying it once wouldn't hurt. She thought she was strong enough to handle it. It never occurred to her that she might be wrong, that addiction might run in her family

Depression, anxiety, escape, curiosity, and boredom are all reasons people start to use meth. Like Alyssa, they kid themselves into believing they can control it. Once they've experienced the euphoric high, though, they want to feel it again and again. Some people become addicted after their first try. Others lose control after a while. They may want to quit, but they can't.

Here are a few other reasons people start using meth:

◆ Athletes and students use it to increase their energy and improve performance.

DONATIONS

Doing volunteer work is a great way to have a fun, positive experience with your friends or family.

◆ Some people use it so they can work extra shifts.

◆ Young women often use it to lose weight.

◆ Teens use it to fit in with their friends.

Some people try meth for recreational reasons. They hear it's a great way to have fun at dances and parties. Others like the feeling of power and confidence it gives them. Also, meth is cheap and easily available, unlike other drugs.

So what do you do if you're tempted to try meth? You could start by asking yourself why. Are you trying to be cool? Do you want to do better in school or sports? Are you feeling stressed by problems at home or at school? Or are you simply looking for a way to rebel?

Some people think that meth will solve all their problems. But meth isn't a wonder drug. It makes you "think" you've solved your problems, but it only makes them worse and leads to addiction. People who use meth know their real problems started after they used the drug. Worried about something in your life? Try talking to an adult you can trust—a parent, a teacher, a friend, or a relative. The only way to solve a problem is to face it, whether or not it's through counseling.

Meanwhile, there are lots of ways for kids to release their frustrations and have fun—healthy fun. You can try out for a sport, join a club, read a book, or watch a movie with a friend. What about volunteering? You could tutor a younger student or walk dogs for the local animal shelter. Activities like these will make you friends, reduce stress, help you relax, and keep you from getting bored.

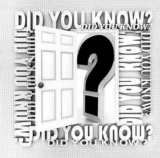

HOW TO
Say "No"

What do you do if someone offers you some meth? Why not try some of these ideas:

◆ Say "No thanks," and walk away.

◆ Give an excuse. "My dad just called me" or "Sorry, I have an appointment today."

◆ Make a joke. "I can't afford to lose any more brain cells."

◆ Change the subject. "I feel like shooting baskets instead."

◆ Your best bet? Avoid situations that involve drugs.

It's a good idea to practice these techniques with your friends so it's easier when you find yourself in a tough situation. Your friends probably feel the same way as you about meth. Practicing with them will give you all more confidence to say "No."

Meth is a Family Affair

One of the saddest consequences of meth abuse is the impact it has on families. Meth addicts lie to their families and even steal from them. When an addict disappears for hours, or even days, at a time, family members are consumed with worry. At first, they may make excuses for the addict, giving her money or bailing him out of jail. When addicts get angry and aggressive, though, families become afraid. They also live in constant fear that the addict will end up in the hospital or, even worse, die. Family members can become as obsessed with the addict as the addict is with meth.

When the addicts are parents, their spouses may doubt themselves. They feel hurt, ashamed, and overwhelmed. They also worry about protecting the children. Family conflicts occur frequently. Some spouses try to "fix" the situation by taking on more responsibility. Children are at risk for depression and alcohol abuse, too. Financial security is often an issue, since many addicts lose their jobs and spend their money on drugs.

When the addict is a son or a daughter, families go to pieces. Parents may argue with each other about how to handle the situation. So much attention goes to the addict that siblings are often neglected or blamed for being a bad example to the addict. Money can also be an issue, because the cost of rehab is high.

If someone in your family is a meth addict, know that you aren't the cause of his or her addiction. Preaching, lecturing, or making threats won't help. Learn the facts of meth addiction. Join a support group or seek professional

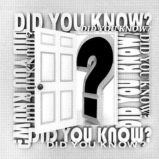

GROWING UP
with Meth

Home life for kids whose parents both use meth is constant chaos. Children go hungry for days at a time. Shopping, making meals, doing laundry, and having an adult's guidance—they all take a back seat to drugs. Parents don't provide medical or dental care. Older kids become caretakers of younger children and their parents.

Children who live in home meth labs suffer the most. They show up at school with burns on their bodies from exposure to toxic chemicals. They inhale secondhand smoke from meth and even absorb the chemicals through their skin from contaminated surfaces, including carpeting, clothing, and furniture. The children often end up in foster homes or living with relatives.

help. You can't rescue an addict. An addict needs to rescue himself. The sooner he can recognize he has a problem, the sooner he's ready for treatment.

Meth and a Teen Brain

The best way to stay out of trouble with meth is to avoid it at all costs. If you have used it, though, the sooner you get help the better, especially if you're a teen. Remember that work in progress—the teen brain? Studies have proven that meth affects the brain, but no one knows for certain the kind of damage it does to a brain that's still developing.

Meth causes dopamine to flood the nerve cells in the brain. Does it interfere with the development of these nerve cells in teens? Meth alters people's perceptions. Does it get in the way of developing a teen's perceptual skills? Meth is habit-forming. Do these meth habits become ingrained in the wiring of a teen's brain? Will all this affect a teen's ability to think, perceive, or reason for the rest of his life? These issues are still being studied. One thing is for sure: Early intervention and treatment offer the best chance of success.[3]

Can People Recover from Meth?

The answer is yes, but recovery doesn't happen overnight. Meth addiction is difficult to treat, especially for chronic users. After forty-five days sober, many addicts hit a wall of depression and may relapse. Some of the effects of meth use—weak memory, inability to concentrate, poor decision-making skills—make it difficult for addicts to

Therapy can be a part of a recovery program.

follow directions. It takes a year or longer for them to learn to control their impulses and stay focused.

Detox is the process of ridding the body of a drug and needs to occur before treatment can begin. It can be done as inpatient or outpatient. Withdrawal symptoms last about two weeks. They include fatigue, hunger, depression, and trouble with memory and reasoning. Outpatient detox needs to be structured and scheduled. Since meth addicts often have health issues that accompany their dependency, they need a medical evaluation and treatment first if they're going to be successful in fighting their addiction.

Rehab treatment should be intense, from three months to a year, and away from access to meth. The best rehab for teens is geared to their specific age. Peer support, age-appropriate therapy, and family support are important. Parents and siblings are often asked to participate in discussion groups and family counseling.

Support groups are a vital part of the recovery process, during rehab and after. Even after a year of rehab, many addicts relapse and have to enter rehab again. Besides being a source of guidance and encouragement, support groups are a safe place to go when you feel challenged. Connecting with others who understand what you're going through can help you feel less afraid and alone. Support groups aren't just for recovering addicts, either. Families and friends of addicts have their own programs where they share experiences and get advice. To learn more about these programs, go to For

Methamphetamine makes the user feel good while he or she is high. However, when the effects of the drug wear off, the user can feel down and depressed.

More Information at the back of this book. Some support groups include the following:

◆ Narcotics Anonymous (NA) is a twelve-step program and self-help group for drug addicts in treatment and recovery. New members choose sponsors who are successful in staying drug-free and who give support.

◆ Crystal Meth Anonymous (CMA) is a fellowship of people who have a problem with crystal meth. It has a twelve-step program for spiritual development. The only requirement is a desire to stop using.

◆ Nar-Anon/Nar-Ateen is a twelve-step program for those affected by someone else's addiction. Members share experiences, strengths, and hopes, and are encouraged to grow through service. Nar-Anon sponsors Nar-Ateen, a similar program for teens.

HOPE FOR *the Future*

In 1997, Andre Agassi was a tennis legend. Two years earlier he'd been ranked number one by the Association of Tennis Professionals (ATP). He was engaged to marry movie star Brooke Shields. He was a multi-millionaire. But Andre had a secret: He hated playing tennis, ever since he was a boy. And he was depressed.

From the time Andre was a child, his father Mike had bullied him into playing tennis. His father was obsessed with the sport and trained Andre's older siblings to be tennis stars without success. Andre was his last hope. Mike was determined that someday his son would be ranked number one in the world.

Andre's father bought a house in the desert near Las Vegas, built a tennis court, and created a ball machine

RRIGHTGATE METHAMPHETAMINE

The Name Game

NICKNAMES, or
STREET NAMES, for
methamphetamine

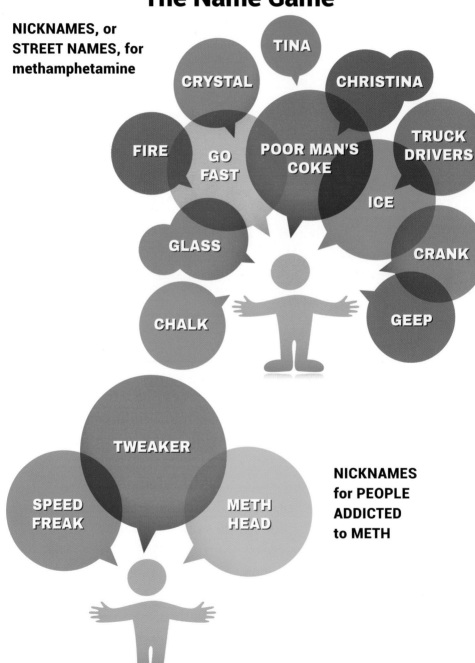

NICKNAMES
for PEOPLE
ADDICTED
to METH

Andre called "the dragon." Andre was only seven. The dragon fired 2,500 balls every day at Andre as his father yelled at him to "hit harder, hit harder."[1] When Andre was thirteen, his father sent him to a tennis academy in Florida. At fourteen, Andre dropped out of school and worked toward becoming a professional tennis player. He played his first professional tournament at sixteen. By the time he was eighteen, he had made over a million dollars in his career and was ranked number three in the world.

Andre was officially a star. In tennis, there are four Grand Slam, or Major, events each year. Andre won his first Grand Slam at Wimbledon when he was twenty-two. At twenty-four, he won the U.S. Open and the Australian Open: two more Grand Slams. By the time he was twenty-five, he had reached the number one rank in the world, a rank that he held for thirty weeks.

Unfortunately, Andre's career went downhill for the next two years. Although he won the gold medal for tennis in the 1996 Olympics, he never made it to any Grand Slam final. He began to question his ability as a player. The fact that a career in tennis had never been his choice began to weigh on him. A wrist injury and his pending marriage to Brooke Shields also worried him. Andre's rank of number one in the world dropped to number 141.

Depressed and withdrawn, Andre found an escape in crystal meth. His assistant Slim suggested that getting high would help. Andre described his first experience, snorting meth with Slim. "There is a moment of regret, followed by a vast sadness. Then comes a tidal wave of euphoria that sweeps away every negative thought in

my head."[2] Andre lost himself to meth for months. He stopped practicing and pulled out of the French Open and Wimbledon. That summer he didn't play tennis at all. Instead, he spent most of his time getting high with Slim.

Andre knew he was harming his body, but he didn't care. He felt happy when he was on meth, even though the physical aftereffects were "hideous."[3] Andre began to compete in a few events, but that fall he got a call from the ATP. He had tested positive for crystal meth. Andre was twenty-seven. His career and reputation were now at stake.

Andre panicked. In a letter to the ATP, he wrote that he'd accidentally drunk a soda that his assistant had laced with meth. He felt guilty about lying, but he was determined to change his life and stop using meth. The ATP didn't suspend him.

Andre now realized how important his career was to him. For the first time in his life, he chose to play tennis for his own sake. Making that choice gave him the strength to stop using meth and turn his career around, winning five titles in the next year. In 1999, he won the French Open, his fourth Grand Slam. Only six other male singles players in history have achieved a Career Grand Slam (winning all four Grand Slam championships). He also ended the year as number one. In 2006, Andre retired from professional tennis. Andre has raised millions for at-risk young people in Southern Nevada. His foundation runs a charter school for them in Las Vegas.

In 2009, Andre Agassi published his autobiography. In it, he admitted to using crystal meth and lying to the ATP.

Andre Agassi recovered from his meth addiction and documented his journey in an autobiography. Agassi is shown here warming up before playing John McEnroe in the Stars Under the Stars gala on July 24, 2010 in Los Angeles.

He said he was ashamed of what he'd done at the time, but couldn't bear the thought of being an outcast because of his stupidity.[4] Andre was lucky. He was able to kick his meth habit and get back on track again. Telling the truth about it may help others avoid making the same mistake.

The Rise and Fall of Meth Use

Crystal meth use in the United States was high during the 1990s when Andre Agassi used it. The good news is that it's declined by over 50 percent nationally since 2006, especially among young people. Some areas of the country still have serious meth problems, though—Hawaii, the West Coast, and the Midwest. Ten states in these areas accounted for over 60 percent of the meth addicts admitted for treatment in 2009 and 2010.

There are other reasons to worry. Meth use tends to rise and fall from year to year. Why? It depends on three things: how available it is, how pure, and how cheap. When the government restricted sales of chemicals used to make meth in 2005, less of the drug became available. It was also not as pure because the meth labs diluted it to make it go further. The price went up and meth use went down. This has been the pattern with meth for the past few decades.

Government restrictions didn't stop the meth labs though. Mexican producers found other sources for needed chemicals. In 2009, they also started manufacturing meth with P2P again. Better techniques produced a meth that was very pure. In 2010, meth entering the United States

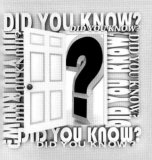

METH LABS—
THE COST TO THE *Environment*

Meth labs are bad for people. Explosions and fires injure or kill addicts, families, law enforcement officers, and firemen. Toxic chemicals used to make meth enter people's bodies and damage the nervous system. But did you know meth labs are also bad for the environment?

Every pound of meth manufactured creates five to six pounds of toxic waste. Super labs can produce hundreds of pounds. Where does it go? Some may be thrown into a backyard where it stays in the soil and pollutes the ground-water for years. Other toxic waste is dumped into rivers, lakes, fields, or sewage systems, which can contaminate water resources for humans and animals. Cleanup of these areas is extremely difficult and expensive.

from the Far East was almost 96 percent pure! Meth was more available, purer, and its use went up.[5]

The Government's Fight Against Meth

In 2009, the Rand Corporation did a study based on data from 2005 that estimated the cost of meth use at 23.4 billion dollars. The study included costs for treatment, health care, premature death, crime, loss of work, child abuse, foster care, and the cost to society for meth labs. What is our government doing about it?

The Office of National Drug Control Policy tackles meth abuse with a balanced approach, including law enforcement, prevention, and treatment.

- ◆ In 2009, government funds helped to dismantle nearly 1,400 meth labs in areas with high drug trafficking.

- ◆ In 2011, law enforcement officers disrupted or dissolved 612 drug trafficking organizations in the United States.

- ◆ The National Youth Anti-Drug Media Campaign raises public awareness of meth abuse through advertising and provides information on meth, its prevention, and treatment.

- ◆ Criminals driven by substance abuse disorders are being diverted from prison to treatment programs that are far less costly.

- ◆ The Affordable Care Act will make drug treatment a required benefit for any Americans who suffer from substance abuse disorders.

Meth Prevention

Since youth is often when people first try drugs, it's important for young people to get accurate information about meth and its dangers. Benjamin Franklin once wrote, "An investment in knowledge pays the best interests." Knowing about meth and how to deal with it is a great payoff. That's because good prevention programs don't just educate you about meth and other drugs. They show you how to live your life successfully without them.

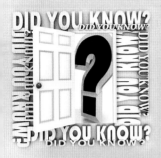

TEENS WITH AN OPINION—
About Meth

Despite what we know about the dangers of meth, some teens still don't take them seriously. The 2010 Georgia Meth Use and Attitudes Study looked at over 2,400 teens and 314 young adults who had recently graduated from high school. Although most teens didn't approve of meth use, a third saw "little or no risk" in using it. Some saw mainly the benefits. Here are some results from the study:

◆ Twenty-one percent believed it helped you lose weight.

◆ Seventeen percent believed it gave you energy.

◆ Nineteen percent believed it made you feel very happy.

◆ Thirty-nine percent said their friends wouldn't give them a hard time if they used meth.

◆ Fifty-eight percent said they had never discussed meth with their parents.[6]

Unfortunately, the so-called benefits of meth are short-lived. So are they really "benefits"? Once the "feel good" aspect wears off, the "feel bad" aspects kick in: restlessness, irritability, insomnia, violence, and eventual mental imbalance. Is it worth risking your health for that?

Below are three examples of successful prevention programs. These programs vary depending on their audience: young people who've never used meth, young people who are at risk for meth use, and young people who've used meth and show signs of addiction.

School-based prevention programs focus on academics but also teach social skills. Kids learn how to work on relationships with friends, develop self-control and coping skills, and assert themselves when someone tries to talk them into doing something they don't want to do.

Family-based prevention programs help parents bond with their kids by teaching them to be supportive and communicate better. They educate parents about drugs and show them how to discuss and enforce policies about drug abuse in a positive way.

Community-based prevention programs work with civic groups, law enforcement, churches, and government agencies to get the message out about the dangers of meth. They might also run a media campaign or community awareness program.

You can't talk about education without mentioning the Internet. Here are three Web sites that teach kids about meth. Web addresses for these sites are at the end of the book.

◆ **NIDA for Teens** is an online source about meth and other drug use, including its causes and effects and other interesting science-based facts. It's available in English and Spanish.

♦ **The Meth Project**'s Web site includes videos, animation, quizzes, frequently asked questions, and personal stories from meth users, their families, and friends. Teens can get help or learn how to take action against meth use.

♦ **Above the Influence** is an interactive site that makes kids more aware of the influences on them to experience drugs.

Treatment for Meth

Meth addiction was once considered untreatable, but studies show it's no longer true. Many factors go into why someone is an addict. The best treatments give equal time to all sides of addiction—mental, emotional, and physical. The biggest obstacle? Convincing addicts they need treatment.

Screening: To convince addicts to get treatment, the National Institute for Drug Abuse recommends a tool for doctors called SBIRT. It stands for screening, brief intervention, and referral for treatment. Screening helps the doctor understand how severe the problem is and what kind of treatment would be best. During a brief intervention the addict is educated about meth abuse and urged to get treatment. The referral step helps the addict find the right kind of treatment.

Inpatient vs. Outpatient Treatment: Inpatient treatment is for people with serious or long-term addiction. For a month to three months or longer, people live in a residence where they take part in therapy, group counseling, and other recovery programs. Outpatient

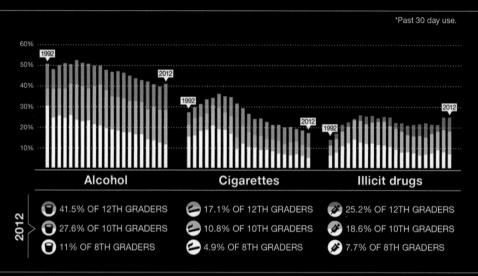

LAST TWO DECADES OF ALCOHOL, CIGARETTE, AND ILLICIT DRUG USE*

*Past 30 day use.

Alcohol   Cigarettes   Illicit drugs

41.5% OF 12TH GRADERS   17.1% OF 12TH GRADERS   25.2% OF 12TH GRADERS

27.6% OF 10TH GRADERS   10.8% OF 10TH GRADERS   18.6% OF 10TH GRADERS

11% OF 8TH GRADERS   4.9% OF 8TH GRADERS   7.7% OF 8TH GRADERS

NIH — National Institute on Drug Abuse

The National Institute on Drug Abuse is a component of the National Institutes of Health, U.S. Department of Health and Human Services. NIDA supports most of the world's research on the health aspects of drug abuse and addiction. Fact sheets on the health effects of drugs of abuse and information on NIDA research and other activities can be found at www.drugabuse.gov.

treatment is for people with less serious meth problems. They go to treatment during the day, but return home at night.

Cognitive Behavioral Therapy (CBT): This treatment works on the theory that bad thinking leads to bad behavior. It focuses on changing people's thoughts in order to change their behavior. Addicts learn why they use meth and how people and situations trigger them. They also learn practical ways to avoid cravings and to deal with them when they occur.

Contingency Management: There's nothing better than getting a "prize" for doing something well. It works for addicts, too. Therapists use positive reinforcement to reward people for meeting treatment goals. A contingency is something that depends on something else happening first. For instance, an addict who has a clean drug test may be rewarded with movie tickets or a meal in a favorite restaurant.

The Matrix Model: This successful outpatient approach combines behavioral therapy with family education, individual counseling, twelve-step support programs, and drug testing. People are also encouraged to get involved in non-drug-related activities.

Education: Addicts are more likely to stay in treatment if they learn about meth, its effect on the body and brain, the ins and outs of meth addiction, and relapse and recovery, as well as the physical, chemical, and psychological effects of staying clean.

Working Together

The problem of meth abuse can't be solved by one person, one group, one treatment, or one program. Meth abuse can be a chronic life-long illness for some addicts. Many people in recovery fight a daily battle to stay on top of their addiction. Unlike asthma or diabetes, it's a disease people choose, even if they don't realize it at the time. Making a smart choice for you is a beginning.

Chapter Notes

Chapter 1
THE "SPEED" Drug

1. David Sheff, *Beautiful Boy* (New York: Houghton Mifflin, 2008), Kindle e-book.
2. Ibid.
3. Ibid.
4. John Bonifield, "Relapse a Constant Threat, 'Tweak' Author Says," *CNN.com*, April 16, 2009, <www.cnnstudentnews.cnn .com> (December 12, 2012).
5. Ibid.
6. PBS.org, "The Meth Epidemic," WGBH Educational Foundation and Oregon Public Broadcasting, <www.pbs .org/wgbh/pages/frontline> (January 22, 2013).
7. L.D. Johnston et al., "Monitoring the Future: National Results on Adolescent Drug Use, Overview of Key Findings, 2011," Ann Arbor: Institute for Social Research, The University of Michigan, <monitoringthefuture.org/pubs/ monographs/mtf-overview2011.pdf> (January 22, 2013).
8. "Drug Facts: Drug-Related Hospital Emergency Room Visits," National Institute on Drug Abuse, <www.drugabuse .gov> (January 22, 2013).

Chapter 2
A DRUG Gone Wrong

1. Nicolas Rasmussen, *On Speed: The Many Lives of Amphetamine* (New York: New York University Press, 2008), Kindle e-book.

2. Dana Hunt, Ph.D., Sarah Kuck, and Linda Truitt, Ph.D., "Methamphetamine Use: Lessons Learned," *National Criminal Justice Reference Service*, February 2006, <www.ncjrs.gov/pdffiles1/nij/grants/209730.pdf> (January 6, 2013).

Chapter 3 — DANGER: *Speed Trap!*

1. "Boy Dies from Drinking Meth at Border Crossing," *CNS News*, January 15, 2014, <www.cnsnews.com/news/article/boy-dies-drinking-meth-border-crossing> (January 26, 2014).
2. Ibid.
3. "Teenager Dies After Drinking '90 Percent Pure' Liquid Meth at U.S. Border Crossing after Trying to Prove to Immigration Officials That It Was Just Juice," *Mail Online*, November 21, 2013, <www.dailymail.co.uk/news/article-2511201> (January 26, 2014).
4. PBS.org, "The Meth Epidemic," WGBH Educational Foundation and Oregon Public Broadcasting, <www.pbs.org/wgbh/pages/frontline> (January 22, 2013).
5. KCI.org, *The Anti-Meth Site*, "Methamphetamine FAQ," <kci.org/meth_info/faq_meth.htm> (December 27, 2012).

Chapter 4 — THE METH *Effect*

1. Kimberly Wollenburg, *Crystal Clean: A Mother's Struggle with Meth Addiction and Recovery* (CreateSpace Independent Publishing Platform, 2012), Kindle e-book, (December 12, 2012).

2. Ibid.

3. "Faces of Meth," Multnomah County Sheriff's Office, Portland, Oregon, <www.facesofmeth.us> (January 20, 2013).

4. Wollenburg.

5. Ibid

6. "Prenatal Methamphetamine Exposure Linked with Problems," National Institute on Drug Abuse, December 21, 2012, <wwwdrugabuse.gov> (January 21, 2013).

7. "Pregnant Teens & Substance Abuse Treatment," *SAMHSA News*, March/April, 2012, Volume 18, Number 2, <www.samhsa.gov/samhsanewsletter/Volume_18_ Number_2/ PregnantTeens.aspx> (January 20, 2012).

8. Karen P. Tandy, "Two Hundred and Seven Million in Drug Money Seized in Mexico City," Drug Enforcement Administration, March 20, 2007, <www.justice.gov/dea/ divisions> (January 20, 2012).

9. KCI.org, The Anti-Meth Site, "When Does It Become Rock Bottom?" <www.kci.org/meth_info/msg_board_ posts/041506> (January 22, 2012).

Chapter 5 — SAYING "NO" to Meth

1. Author Unknown, "My Life on Meth," *L.A. Youth*, September 2008.

2. Ibid.

3. Daniel R. Weinberger, M.D., Brita Elvevag, Ph.D., Jay N. Giedd, M.D., "The Adolescent Brain: A Work in Progress," *The National Campaign to Prevent Teen Pregnancy*, June 2005, <http://www.thenationalcampaign.org/resources/pdf/ brain.pdf> (January 15, 2013).

HOPE FOR the Future

1. Andre Agassi, *Open: An Autobiography*, (New York: Alfred A. Knopf, 2010), p. 29.
2. Ibid., p. 243.
3. Ibid., p. 248.
4. Ibid., p. 255.
5. Jane Carlisle Maxwell, Ph.D., and Mary-Lyn Brecht, Ph.D., "Methamphetamine: Here We Go Again?" US National Library of Medicine, Epub, July 22, 2011, Addictive Behaviors, December 2011, <http://www.ncbi.nlm.nih.gov/pmc/articles/PMC3243901>(January 30, 2013).
6. Andria Simmons, "Teen Attitudes on Meth Are Surprising," *The Atlanta Journal-Constitution*, March 9, 2010, <http://www.ajc.com/news/news/local/teen-attitudes-on-meth-are-surprising/nQdBk/> (January 30, 2013).

Glossary

addiction—A brain disease that causes an uncontrollable dependence on a substance or behavior.

adrenaline—A hormone produced in the body during times of stress or danger. When produced synthetically, it's used to treat cardiac arrest, asthma, and other problems.

amphetamine—A stimulant drug with legal uses. It's highly addictive when misused or used illegally.

Benzedrine—An amphetamine once commonly used for weight loss, nasal congestion, and depression.

binge—A long run of uninterrupted meth use. People are hyperactive and rarely sleep, but keep taking meth to avoid crashing.

cognitive behavioral therapy—An addiction treatment that focuses on changing people's thoughts in order to change their behavior.

compulsion—An overwhelming urge to perform an act, often repetitively.

contingency management—An addiction treatment that rewards people for meeting treatment goals.

crank—An impure form of meth that is mixed with other substances. Also another street name for meth.

crash—The comedown when someone suddenly stops using meth. Addicts often sleep for days and feel depressed or suicidal.

crystal—Meth in rock form; also called ice.

Desoxyn—The legal, prescription form of methamphetamine.

detox—The abbreviation for "detoxification," or withdrawing from a drug under medical supervision.

dopamine—The "feel good" chemical in the brain that makes people feel pleasure.

ephedra—A plant-based drug used for weight loss and energy. Once available over the counter, it was banned in 2003 because it caused heart problems and strokes.

ephedrine—A stimulant drug used legally to treat allergies and asthma. It's a key ingredient in meth.

euphoria—Extreme happiness, excitement, or feeling of well-being.

hallucination—The seeing, hearing, or sensing what isn't there.

high—A state of euphoria caused by drugs.

hyperthermia—A very high body temperature. Meth overdose can cause this possibly fatal condition.

ma huang—The Chinese name for the ephedra plant.

Matrix Model—An addiction therapy that combines outpatient behavioral therapy with family education, individual counseling, twelve-step support programs, and drug testing.

methamphetamine—A highly addictive stimulant drug in the amphetamine family that is manufactured and obtained illegally.

meth hangover—Period after a crash when the meth addict is mentally and physically exhausted, starved, and dehydrated. Addicts who aren't in rehab usually go back to taking meth to "cure" themselves.

overdose—An excessive amount of a drug, more than the body can handle. Meth overdose can cause hyperthermia, heart attack, coma, and death.

P2P—An abbreviation of phenyl-2-propanone, an ingredient used to make meth before 1980. It is now strictly controlled by the government.

Pervitan—The name used for methamphetamine in the Czech Republic and other parts of Eastern Europe. The drug was used by the Germans during World War II.

process addiction—Addiction to a behavior, like gambling or shopping.

pseudoephedrine—A stimulant drug in the amphetamine family. It's a key ingredient in meth.

rehab—Short for "rehabilitation." An inpatient or outpatient program for drug addicts after detox. It helps them learn to live without the drug and involves counseling and support groups.

reward pathway—The nerve pathway in the brain that controls motivation, behavior, and pleasure. Addictive drugs can short-circuit this pathway.

SBIRT—Acronym for screening, brief intervention, and referral for treatment. A tool doctors use to convince addicts to get treatment.

schedule II drug—A drug that has a strong possibility of abuse or addiction but also has medical uses.

snort—To inhale an illegal drug through the nose.

speed—A street name for amphetamines, because the drugs speed up the central nervous system.

stimulant—A drug that speeds up the central nervous system and makes people alert and energetic.

substance addiction—Addiction to a thing, like drugs or alcohol.

super labs—Big, factory-type meth labs that produce tons of meth. Most of these are found in Mexico and California.

synapse—The space between nerves.

synthetic drug—A drug that does not occur in nature and is produced artificially.

tolerance—The point where a drug stops making a person feel high or even very good. It occurs with repeated use.

toxic—Poisonous, harmful, or deadly.

tweaking—The repetitive behaviors meth addicts engage in; also the crazy, dangerous behavior of a meth addict who's bingeing.

uppers—Stimulant drugs that increase mental alertness and physical function.

For More Information

Organizations

Crystal Meth Anonymous
4470 W Sunset Blvd, Suite 107 PMB 555
Los Angeles, CA 90027-6302
(855) 638-4383
<http://www.crystalmeth.org/>

Nar-Anon Family Groups
22527 Crenshaw Boulevard, Suite 200B
Torrance, CA 90505
(800) 477-6291
<http://www.nar-anon.org>

Narcotics Anonymous
78 Gough Street
San Francisco, CA 94102
(415) 621-8600
<http://www.na.org/>

National Institute on Drug Abuse (NIDA)
Office of Science Policy and
Communication, Public Information and
Liaison Branch
6001 Executive Boulevard
Room 5213, MSC 9561
Bethesda, MD 20892-9561
(301) 443-1124
<http://www.drugabuse.gov/>

Office of National Drug Control Policy
The White House
1600 Pennsylvania Avenue NW
Washington, DC 20500
(202) 456-1414
<http://www.whitehouse.gov/ondcp/>

Substance Abuse and Mental Health Services Administration (SAMHSA)
1 Choke Cherry Road
Rockville, MD 20857
(877) 726-4727
<http://www.samhsa.gov/>

Further Reading

Books

Kuhn, Cynthia, Scott Swartzwelder and Will Wilson. *Buzzed: The Straight Facts About the Most Used and Abused Drugs from Alcohol to Ecstasy.* New York: W. W. Norton & Company, 2014

Norquist, Lara and Frank Spalding. *The Truth About Methamphetamine and Crystal Meth.* New York: Rosen Publishing Group, 2011.

Office of National Drug Control. *Methamphetamine: Crystal Meth— Abuse, Addiction and Treatments.* Washington, D.C.: Office of National Drug Control, 2014.

Sheff, David. *Beautiful Boy: A Father's Journey Through His Son's Addiction.* New York: Houghton Mifflin, 2008.

Sheff, Nic. *Tweak: Growing Up on Methamphetamines.* New York: Atheneum Books for Young Readers, 2008.

Wollenburg, Kimberly. *Crystal Clean: A Mother's Struggle with Meth Addiction and Recovery.* CreateSpace Independent Publishing Platform, 2012 or <info@crystalclean.com>

Internet Addresses

Frontline: The Meth Epidemic. WGBH Educational Foundation. © 2006, 2011.
   <http://www.pbs.org/wgbh/pages/frontline/meth>

National Institute on Drug Abuse (NIDA). *NIDA for Teens.* © 2013.
   <http://teens.drugabuse.gov/>

The Meth Project. Meth Project Foundation, Inc. © 2014.
   <http://www.methproject.org/>

Index